Juliette Kinzie

Badger Biographies

Juliette Kinzie

Frontier Storyteller

KATHE CROWLEY CONN

WISCONSIN HISTORICAL SOCIETY PRESS

Published by the Wisconsin Historical Society Press
Publishers since 1855

© 2015 by the State Historical Society of Wisconsin

For permission to reuse material from *Juliette Kinzie: Frontier Storyteller* (ISBN 978-0-87020-701-3, e-book ISBN 978-0-87020-702-0), please access www.copyright.com or contact the Copyright Clearance Center, Inc. (CCC), 222 Rosewood Drive, Danvers, MA 01923, 978-750-8400. CCC is a not-for-profit organization that provides licenses and registration for a variety of users.

wisconsinhistory.org

Photographs identified with WHi or WHS are from the Society's collections; address requests to reproduce these photos to the Visual Materials Archivist at the Wisconsin Historical Society, 816 State Street, Madison, WI 53706.

Front cover: This portrait of Juliette was painted by the artist G. P. A. Healy when Juliette was about 50 years old, around the time *Wau-Bun* was published. Reprinted with permission from Girl Scouts of the USA.

Printed in Wisconsin USA
Designed by Jill Bremigan

19 18 17 16 15   1 2 3 4 5

Library of Congress Cataloging-in-Publication Data

Conn, Kathe Crowley.
  Juliette Kinzie : frontier storyteller / Kathe Crowley Conn.—1st edition.
     pages cm. — (Badger biographies)
  Includes bibliographical references and index.
  Audience: Grades 4-6.
  ISBN 978-0-87020-701-3 (pbk. : alk. paper) — ISBN 978-0-87020-702-0 (e-book) 1. Kinzie, John H., Mrs., 1806-1870. 2. Frontier and pioneer life—Wisconsin—Juvenile literature. 3. Pioneer women—Wisconsin—Biography. 4. Indian agents—Wisconsin—Biography—Juvenile literature. 5. Ho Chunk Indians—Juvenile literature. 6. Wisconsin—Biography—Juvenile literature. I. Title.
  F584.C66 2014
  977.5'03092—dc23
  [B]
                              2014038701

∞ The paper used in this publication meets the minimum requirements of the American National Standard for Information Sciences—Permanence of Paper for Printed Library Materials, ANSI Z39.48-1992.

To Juliette and the quest for adventure in every young person's life; and to my husband Jeff and daughters Sarah and Emily for going along with the ride.

Contents

1

Meet Juliette

Imagine moving to a new place far away from home. What if you didn't have the things that help you feel comfortable and safe? How would you feel if the land and people were so different that you needed guides and **interpreters** to help find your way?

In the early 1800s, Juliette Magill Kinzie grew up in a comfortable home in **Connecticut**. As a young girl, Juliette dreamed of adventure. When Juliette was 24 years old, she moved to a place called Fort **Winnebago**, in a land once known as the **Northwest Territory**. Part of this land would later become Wisconsin.

interpreter (in **tur** pruh tur): a person who turns spoken words of one language into a different language
Connecticut: kuh **net** uh kuht   **Winnebago**: win uh **bay** goh   **Northwest Territory**: a large part of the United States that once included all or parts of Indiana, Illinois, Michigan, Wisconsin, and Minnesota

A postcard showing what Fort Winnebago looked like in 1834

Wisconsin's History as a US Territory

The large area known as the Northwest Territory included all or parts of 5 present-day states: Indiana, Illinois, Michigan, Wisconsin, and Minnesota. Over time, people began to move from the settled East Coast to these new territories. As people moved in, the names used to describe the land began to shift.

Wisconsin was one of the last areas in the Northwest Territory to be settled. During this time, Wisconsin was known by many different names.

In 1800, the land we now call Wisconsin was part of the Indiana Territory. In 1809, the boundaries shifted and the land was part of the Illinois Territory. In 1818, after Illinois became a state, the boundaries shifted again. What we call Wisconsin today became part of the Michigan Territory.

When Juliette arrived in 1830, Fort Winnebago was part of the Michigan Territory. In 1836, as the population grew, it became known as the Wisconsin Territory. Then in 1848, 18 years after Juliette arrived, Wisconsin officially became a state.

Juliette arrived at Fort Winnebago in 1830. There were few towns or roads on the **frontier**. There were none of the **conveniences** we enjoy today. Imagine looking out your bedroom window and seeing nothing but forests or prairie for as far as you could see. Your nearest neighbor might live many miles away.

This is what the land looked like to Juliette. It was a place where people had to protect themselves from the weather and wild animals. They had to grow or hunt most of their food. And they had to depend on the help of other people to survive.

frontier (fruhn **tir**): the edge of a settled part of a country   convenience (kuhn **vee** nyuns): personal comfort

Juliette and her husband, John Kinzie, lived among the other early **settlers** who worked at Fort Winnebago. Very few female settlers lived on the frontier in 1830. But Juliette was excited by the promise of new lands and adventures.

When Juliette arrived, she believed the frontier would be wild and unsettled. But she quickly learned the land had been home to Indian peoples for thousands of years.

Juliette and John moved to the frontier during a very troubling time. In the 1830s, the US government was removing Indians from their lands so the United States could **expand**. During Juliette's time on the frontier, she made friends with the other settlers, as well as the Indians who visited and lived around the fort. She learned about their **cultures**, **customs**, and love of the land. And she came to believe they had the right to practice their own beliefs and ways of life.

Juliette and John lived at Fort Winnebago for only 3 years. But it was a time of great change. The landscape as Juliette knew it was beginning to disappear, as new towns and roads

settler: a person who comes to live in a new region   **expand**: to grow or increase in size   **culture**: the habits, beliefs, and traditions of a particular people, place, or time   **custom**: the usual way of doing things

were built. And the ways of life for both Indians and settlers were quickly changing, too.

Juliette knew she was witnessing an important part of history. She wanted to make sure no one forgot about the lives of the Indians and settlers. She knew it was important to share her story in her own words: what she saw, what she thought, and what she learned. She wanted other people to learn from her experiences.

Juliette was one of the few people from that time to write down what was happening in that part of the country. Many years later, she wrote a book about her life on the frontier called ***Wau-Bun**: The Early Day in the North-West.*

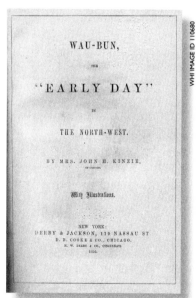

The title page of *Wau-Bun*. If you wrote a book about your life, what would it be called?

Juliette also wrote letters to other people who could help her **document** this important history. One person she wrote to was a man named **Lyman** Draper.

Wau-Bun: waw buhn   **document:** record the details about   **Lyman:** lı muhn

5

Mr. Draper was busy forming the new State Historical Society of Wisconsin. He was interested in collecting stories from **pioneers**. Mr. Draper created one of the most important collections of historical documents in the country.

WHI IMAGE ID 2629

Juliette wrote letters to Mr. Draper, describing the Indian leaders and the early days in Wisconsin and northern Illinois. Today these letters are very valuable. They show us how people viewed their world in the early days of the United States.

Lyman Draper, the first director of the Wisconsin Historical Society.

Much of what we know about Juliette Kinzie and her life comes from her letters and what she wrote in *Wau-Bun*. Juliette teaches us that everyone can have an important story to tell. It doesn't matter whether we are young or old, rich or poor, girl or boy.

This is Juliette's story.

pioneer: a person who is one of the first to settle in an area or to do something new

2

Growing Up in Connecticut

When Juliette Augusta Magill was born in 1806, the United States was a much smaller country. Today we have 50 states. But when Juliette was born, there were only 17 states. These states were located along the eastern coast, where many people had settled.

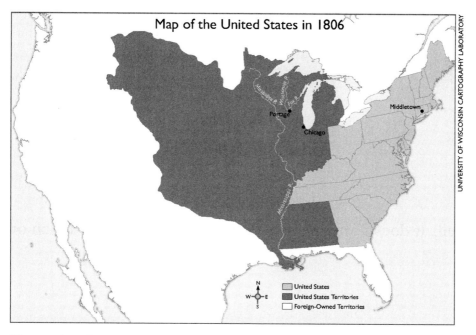

Map of the United States in 1806

This is what the United States looked like when Juliette was born.

Life was very different in Juliette's time. Imagine a world where there were no cars or trucks and only a few roads. People walked, rode horses, or drove wagons across the land. Many villages were located along lakes and rivers. Sometimes the only way you could reach them was by taking a boat across the water.

Electricity had not yet been discovered. Even in the wealthiest towns, homes were lit by candlelight. Chores like washing clothes and cleaning were done by hand. It took people much longer to do the things we do quickly today.

There were no grocery stores or refrigerators, so food was picked and prepared fresh every day or stored in cellars for winter.

There were no movies, television, radio, or Internet. In the evenings, families would read aloud, tell stories, or sing and make music together.

Middletown, Connecticut, where Juliette grew up

Most families lived on farms, but some people lived in towns and cities. Juliette lived with her mother, father, and siblings in a city called Middletown. It was one of the largest and wealthiest cities in Connecticut.

Middletown had a large town park, several roads, a town hall, and fancy churches. The residents of Middletown were very proud of their city.

Families in Middletown valued their nice homes, fancy furniture, and fine belongings of silver and china. They believed these items gave them **social status** and **prestige**.

In cities like Middletown, there were social rules and expectations that governed what people did and how they acted. Young women and men were taught proper **etiquette** and manners. These rules were part of Juliette's culture.

There were also strict rules about what men and women could do when they grew up. Men were expected to learn a skill or go to college. Many young women were not allowed to go to school. They were expected to stay home and take care of their families.

But young Juliette wanted something different. When she was 15, Juliette attended a new school started by a woman named Emma Willard. The school was called the Troy Female Seminary. It was one of the first schools in the country designed just for girls. At Miss Willard's school, Juliette could learn subjects that were usually taught only to boys and men.

social status: position or rank in a particular society   **prestige** (pre **steezh**): importance or respect gained through success or excellence   **etiquette** (et uh ket): the rules governing the proper way to behave or to do something

10

Emma Willard and the Female Education Movement

When Juliette was born, girls did not go to college. They were not expected to learn many of the subjects that were taught to boys. But a woman named Emma Willard thought differently.

Emma Willard wanted to open a school where girls could learn  subjects like French, Latin, math, and science. She asked the state government of New York to let her start a school for girls.

The state government said no. But Emma Willard would not give up. The people of Troy, New York, liked Emma Willard's ideas. They agreed it was important for girls to be able to go to school, too. The city of Troy helped her establish the new school.

Emma Hart Willard was a pioneer of women's education.

In 1821, Emma Willard opened her school. She called it the Troy Female Seminary. The school still operates today as the Emma Willard School.

With her new schooling and her thirst for adventure, would Juliette be happy following the strict social rules about what girls could and could not do?

Juliette had other ideas.

3

A Partner in Adventure

When Juliette was growing up, it was a special treat to receive letters in the mail. A letter might have to travel by special **messenger** across wild lands, lakes, and rivers. A letter could travel for months before reaching its **destination**.

You can imagine Juliette's excitement when she received a letter from her uncle, who lived far away in Chicago.

Chicago, Illinois, Nov. 6, 1820

Dear Juliette,

   Although it is some time since I received the last two letters from you, I have not yet thanked you for them, but I do it now and with enthusiasm. I hope you will continue to send me

---

messenger: a person who carries a message or does an errand   **destination** (des tuh **nay** shuhn): a place to which a person is going or something is sent

13

more letters, full of the same delightful spirit and humor.

Your letters . . . remind me of the charming gatherings we used to have around your mother's cheerful fireside. I trust those happy times will soon return. Meanwhile, you must devote an occasional letter to your uncle who loves you, and sees with pride and affection the progress you are making in your education.

The letter was signed by her uncle, Dr. Alexander Wolcott.

Several years earlier, Juliette's uncle had left his comfortable home in Connecticut. He moved to a place called Fort Dearborn, which is now in the city of Chicago. He worked as a doctor and an Indian Agent at the fort. He worked with soldiers, fur traders, and Indians, and

Juliette's uncle, Dr. Alexander Wolcott, was an Indian Agent at Fort Dearborn in Chicago.

CHICAGO HISTORY MUSEUM: ICHi-68727

he helped explore the land. He sent long letters to Juliette. He described the people he met, the places he saw, and the challenges of life in what people often called "Indian Country."

In this letter, Juliette's uncle described a boat trip on Lake Superior. He wrote about the huge, jagged rocks that towered over his head. The waves slapped against the rocks. And he heard spooky noises that sounded like they were coming "from the very center of the earth."

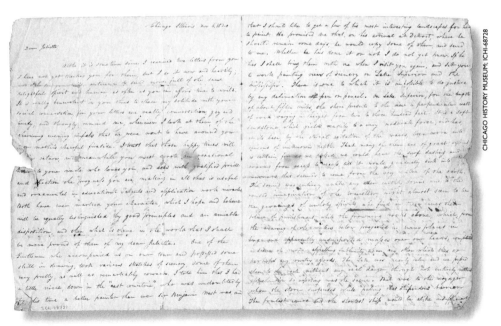

One of the letters Juliette received from her uncle, Alexander Wolcott. This letter describes her uncle's boat trip on Lake Superior.

CHICAGO HISTORY MUSEUM: ICHi-68728

But the lake was also beautiful. Farther along, he discovered a small waterfall where a river spilled into the lake. He wrote to Juliette that it fell "in one unbroken sheet...glittering with all the hues of the rainbow."

What was this magical place, where a traveler could be terrified by spooky sounds one moment and delighted by a glittering waterfall the next? It certainly did not sound like anything Juliette had seen in Middletown, Connecticut!

The letters from her uncle filled Juliette's imagination. She imagined the beauty of the wild lands, the challenges of survival, and the excitement of living with different cultures.

Juliette dreamed of a life of adventure, exploring the wilderness. She looked forward to every single word her uncle sent.

Westward Expansion

In the 1800s, the United States was expanding westward. Towns and farms along the East Coast were filling with settlers from Europe. The United States needed room to grow. The government wanted to build new settlements in the **vast** lands to the west.

If you look at a map of the United States during Juliette's childhood, the western edge of the country stopped at what is now Ohio and Indiana. The people who were settling in the United States were new to this **continent**. They did not know what the land looked like west of the Ohio River.

President Thomas Jefferson wondered if the land to the west would be a good place to expand his growing country. In 1804, he sent a team of explorers to travel there and bring back maps and stories of their discoveries. The explorers were led by Meriwether Lewis and William Clark.

Two years later, Lewis and Clark returned

US explorers Meriwether Lewis (left) and William Clark (right)

---

vast: very large in size or amount   **continent**: one of the great divisions of land on the globe—Africa, Antarctica, Asia, Australia, Europe, North America, or South America with news of forests, lakes, prairies, and majestic mountains. The US government thought it would be a good place to settle. It wanted the land for its own.

However, this land was already home to many different Indian tribes. The Ho-Chunk, **Menominee**, and **Ojibwe** tribes had long lived in what is now Wisconsin. Other tribes lived there, too, after they were forced away from their homes by settlers in the east. These included the **Miami**, **Illinois**, **Potawatomi**, Sauk, Fox, **Kickapoo**, **Oneida**, Brothertown, and Stockbridge-Munsee tribes.

The Indians had their own communities, traditions, and ways of life on these lands before the non-Indian settlers arrived.

Westward expansion threatened the ways of life for many Indian tribes.

Menominee: muh **nom** uh nee   **Ojibwe:** oh **jib** way   **Miami:** mi **am** ee   **Illinois:** il uh **noi**   **Potawatomi:** pot uh **wot** uh mee   **Kickapoo:** **kik** uh poo   **Oneida:** oh **ni** duh

When Juliette was 17 years old, she received exciting news. Her uncle was coming back to her grandparents' home in nearby Boston for a visit.

When Juliette arrived in Boston, she had another surprise. Her uncle brought along a young friend named John Harris Kinzie. John Kinzie was kind and charming. And he was an expert on Indians, wilderness, and frontier life.

As a young boy, John grew up with the Indians and settlers in the area that would later become Chicago. When John was

15 years old, he left to work at a trading post at a place called **Mackinac** Island. While John was there, he learned the languages and customs of the local Indian tribes. He also became a talented violin player. The sound of his beautiful music during the long winters was a treat on the frontier.

John Harris Kinzie

Mackinac: **mak** uh naw

Juliette had met the perfect partner for adventure! Juliette and John fell in love. They were married in her parents' home on August 9, 1830.

Juliette was excited about life with her new husband. Together they would do what Juliette had dreamed of: leave the East Coast and move to John's home on the frontier.

The year before they met, John had started a new job as the Indian Agent at Fort Winnebago. This was the area that would later become Portage, Wisconsin. John's job was to represent the US government to the 5,000 Ho-Chunk and Menominee Indians who lived in the region around Fort Winnebago. He gave out money and supplies to the Indians, explained the government's rules, and helped settle **disputes**.

The Indian Agent's work was serious business, but John also knew how to have fun. The local Indians admired John for his skill at the Indian game of **lacrosse** and for his speed at races.

dispute: an argument or disagreement   **lacrosse** (luh **kraws**): a game played on a field using a long-handled stick with a shallow net for catching, throwing, and carrying the ball

20

Lacrosse began as a popular Indian sport.

John was also curious about how the Indians lived. He was eager to talk with them. John learned at least 6 Indian languages, including Ho-Chunk, **Wyandot**, Potawatomi, Dakotah, Ojibwe, and **Ottawa**. John's relationships with the Indians and his knowledge of the land made him the perfect person for the job.

Wyandot: wi uhn doht   **Ottawa: ot** uh wuh

21

The Job of the Indian Agent

The US government promised to give Indians money and supplies every year if they agreed to move off their land. These promises were written up in formal documents called **treaties**. Someone needed to make sure the treaties were enforced.

To do so, the government hired Indian Agents. The Indian Agent's job was to pass out money and supplies to the Indians and explain the rules of the treaties. Indians visited the Indian Agent each year to receive their payments. Indian Agents were responsible for settling disputes and telling the government about the Indian tribes in their area.

It was important for Indian Agents to understand the local Indian cultures. Some Indian Agents treated the Indians unfairly. But others respected the Indians and their ways of life.

John Kinzie kept the silver money he gave to the Indians safe in this sturdy box.

treaty: an agreement between 2 or more states or groups of people

Juliette and John planned to live near Fort Winnebago, far away from the fine homes and cultured life of Connecticut. Juliette got ready for the move. She packed china, silver, and linens for their dining room. She brought pictures for the walls, fancy wood furniture, and even her big piano! Juliette packed everything into wooden crates. The crates were loaded onto a boat that would take them on their **journey**.

Juliette's childhood home might have had a fancy dining room similar to this one. Juliette packed her fine china and shipped it all the way from Connecticut to Fort Winnebago.

journey: an act of traveling from one place to another

Juliette knew it could be a long and dangerous trip from Connecticut to Fort Winnebago. It was rare for a woman from the East to live so deep in the wilderness. And there were many things she didn't know. Where would they stay? What would they eat? What would her new home be like? How would they survive? What kind of people would they meet? And, being from so far away, would she be accepted in this new land?

Juliette may have thought silently about these questions. But she wanted to prove that as an educated young woman, she could survive on the frontier as well as any man. She focused her thoughts on the adventures ahead of her. After a lifetime of wishing and waiting to explore the frontier, Juliette was about to move to the land of her dreams.

4

Traveling to the New Frontier

Today, if you were moving from Connecticut to Wisconsin, your family might load a moving van, get into a car or airplane, and travel for a day or 2 to your new home.

But in Juliette's day, the trip was much more difficult. Juliette discovered that traveling to her new home would be an adventure of its own!

Travelers often stopped in the wilderness to camp, eat, or stay overnight in remote cabins.

There were no roads in the wilderness. Indians, fur traders, and settlers often traveled long distances by water. They built villages, trading posts, and forts along the rivers and lakes. Travelers could stop there to eat or sleep during their journey.

To reach Fort Winnebago, Juliette and John first traveled to Detroit, Michigan. From Detroit they would take a boat across the Great Lakes. The trip would take 2 weeks.

Their boat was a new and fancy steamboat called the *Henry Clay*. The older sailboats relied on wind to move forward. But if the wind stopped, a sailboat would stop, too. Steamboats were different. They were powered by steam engines and did not rely on the wind.

WHI IMAGE ID 5678

A steamboat, similar to the boat Juliette and John used to cross the Great Lakes

Juliette, John, and the other **passengers** boarded the steamboat and began their journey. The women slept in a room made of canvas

passenger: someone riding on or in a vehicle

26

walls. It was called the Women's Cabin. The men slept in another room called the Men's Cabin.

The first day of the trip was sunny and warm. But on the second day, the sky darkened. Suddenly, rain began to fall. It rained so hard that it leaked through the roof and flooded the Women's Cabin. Their carpet and bedding were ruined! Juliette and the other women ran out of the room to escape the water. The Men's Cabin was dry, so the women went there to stay warm.

Juliette was happy to find shelter. But within minutes, the canvas roof of the Men's Cabin split open. A flood of water rushed in. Everyone was soaked! Quickly they squeezed into the last dry areas on the boat and sat under umbrellas.

Their clothes were wet, and they were cold and uncomfortable. They sang and told stories to cheer themselves up as they waited for the rain to stop. Juliette knew this would not be the first challenge they would face. She told herself it would be important to stay cheerful.

By the end of the second day, the boat came to its first stop. It was Mackinac Island, where John had lived and worked as a young man. Today, Mackinac Island is part of the state of Michigan. It is located at the point where the waters of Lake **Huron** and Lake Michigan meet. The island was named after the Indian word *Michilimackinac*, which meant "the Big Turtle." From a distance, the island looked like a turtle sitting on the water.

Mackinac Island was a busy place. It had a trading post and a fort. Many people traveled to the island to trade food and supplies.

Juliette and John stepped ashore. Juliette was amazed by all the activity! Along the beach were the wigwams of the Ottawa Indians who had come to the island to trade. Juliette looked out at the water. She saw hundreds of small boats coming toward the island, all filled with traders and Indians coming to shore.

The Indians brought items to trade from the West. They brought valuable furs of beaver, otter, mink, fox, wolf, bear,

Huron: hyoor on   **Michilimackinac:** mish uh luh **mak** uh naw

WHI IMAGE ID 10001

Wigwams were sturdy homes made from curved wooden poles often covered in animal hides and rush mats.

wildcat, and muskrat. They also brought food they had gathered, such as maple sugar, corn, beans, and wild rice. Indian women brought items they had carefully made by hand: **moccasins**, mats, hunting pouches, and little boxes made of birch bark and filled with maple sugar. They also brought toy models of Indian cradles, snowshoes, and canoes.

moccasin: **mok** uh suhn

29

The Indians traded these goods with non-Indian traders from the East Coast, Canada, and Europe. The non-Indian traders wanted the animal furs and other items to sell back home.

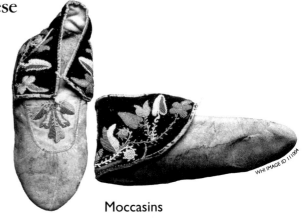

Moccasins

In exchange, the non-Indian traders offered items such as blankets, fabric, kettles, traps, silver items, hand mirrors, and combs.

Many years earlier, French explorers had come to the island. Because of this, many of the Indians knew French words. Juliette was surprised to hear them say "**Bonjour**," which is the French word for "hello."

The Fur Trade

French explorers came to the Great Lakes region in the 1600s. When they arrived, they found Indian tribes hunting animals such as beaver, mink, and otter. Beaver fur was popular for making hats and clothing, especially in France.

bonjour: bohn **zhur**

30

The furs were so popular that the French and French-Canadians built trading posts where they could exchange goods with the Indians. The traders were very successful. Soon the British joined in the fur trade. British and French traders established major trading posts at Fort Michilimackinac and other locations around the Great Lakes.

Other businesses and settlements began to grow around these trading posts. After the **American Revolutionary War**, the US government and companies such as the American Fur Company took control over the trading posts.

The fur trade lasted almost 200 years, until beaver hats became unpopular and the Indians lost control of their hunting grounds.

WHI IMAGE ID 101778

A fur trading post in Fond du Lac, Wisconsin, owned by the American Fur Company

American Revolutionary War: the war for American independence from Great Britain, fought from 1775 to 1783

31

Juliette was also surprised to learn about a local Ottawa woman named Madame **Laframboise**. There were no schools for Indian children on Mackinac Island, so Madame Laframboise started a school in her home. Madame Laframboise's husband worked at a trading post. When he died, Madame Laframboise took over his job. She became a skilled businesswoman and supervised the trading post and its workers.

Juliette was impressed by Madame Laframboise's story. She could do an important job just as well as any man. What a change this was from a woman's life back East!

Juliette did not want to forget her adventures, so she made sketches and took notes on what she saw. After a day on Mackinac Island, Juliette and John boarded the steamboat and continued on their voyage.

The boat traveled across Lake Michigan. Juliette admired the "gigantic forest trees . . . and the little **glades** of prairie" along the shore. Finally, the steamboat arrived at their next destination, Green Bay, which was home to Fort Howard. The passengers got off the boat, ready to stay in Green Bay for the next 2 nights.

Laframboise: lah **frahm** boiz   **glade:** an open space in a forest

WHI IMAGE ID 109889

Juliette wanted to share what she saw with others. She drew many pictures of her travels, like this one. Juliette knew the landscape would be changing. This is where the town of Neenah, Wisconsin, would be formed just a few years later.

Green Bay was an important outpost in the Northwest Territory. When Juliette and John arrived, the town was buzzing with activity. An important treaty was being **negotiated** at Fort Howard, between the US government and several Indian tribes, including the Menominee, Oneida, Stockbridge-Munsee, Saint **Regis**, **Onondaga**, and **Tuscarora** peoples. The town was filled with government officials, Indians, and other visitors. There were so many people, the town's only hotel was full.

negotiated (ni **go** shee ay tid): had a discussion with another person in order to settle something
Regis: **ree** juhs   **Onondaga**: ah nuh **dah** guh   **Tuscarora**: tuhs kuh **rohr** uh

33

Treaties: Who Controls the Land?

The Indians and the US government had different ways of thinking about the land. The Indians hunted, farmed, and lived on the land. They believed the land should be shared. The US government believed differently. They wanted to divide the land and sell it to individuals who would own and control it by themselves.

The government pressured Indians to give up their land in exchange for different land farther west. These agreements were written up in treaties. The government used treaties to limit who could own the lands and waters and who could use them.

The way the government created these treaties was often unfair. The treaties were written in English, which many Indians could not speak or read. Some treaties were signed by tribal members who did not represent the wishes of their communities. And some Indian leaders were angry and did not want to sell their lands at any price.

WHI IMAGE ID 3142

A treaty gathering between territorial governors and members of several Indian tribes. The gathering shown here happened in 1825 in Prairie du Chien, Wisconsin.

People of all different backgrounds hurried to find places to sleep for the night. Strangers shared bedrooms or slept on the floor. Juliette and John were happy to find a room to sleep in. But they had to share the room with a general who was in town for the treaty negotiations. All night, the general read aloud and talked to his soldiers. This made it difficult for Juliette and John to sleep.

The next morning, Juliette and John left the general's room to see the town. They ran into one of John's old friends, a judge named James Duane Doty. The judge invited Juliette and John stay at his house. Juliette was happy to leave the crowded hotel for Judge Doty's cozy home!

One night, friends of Judge Doty and his wife hosted a party for Juliette and John. The town residents came to dance and meet the visitors. Juliette was surprised by how many

different types of people gathered for the party. The rowdy crowd was unlike the fancy parties she had attended with her friends in Connecticut. But she was grateful for the company of strangers and for the advice they offered about living on the frontier. There was so much to learn!

After the party was over Juliette and John were very tired. They were eager to get a good night's sleep at Judge Doty's house.

But as the sun began to rise the next morning, Juliette was startled awake. She heard an unusual noise coming from the room below. It was an **eerie** wail, rising and falling with a **mournful** sound.

What could it be, she wondered? Scared, Juliette woke her husband.

John smiled. He explained it was an Indian man singing his morning prayers and giving thanks for the new day.

Juliette was surprised. At the time, most non-Indian people did not understand the diverse languages and customs of the

eerie (ir ee): causing fear and uneasiness   **mournful**: full of sorrow or sadness

36

different Indian tribes. Some people even called the Indians "wild savages." Juliette was beginning to realize how cruel and untrue that term was. To her, there was something beautiful in the Indian's morning song of praise. She was impressed by the Indian's thoughtfulness.

What a good lesson this Indian could teach non-Indian people, who often forget to be thankful for each day, she thought to herself.

The Kinzies prepared to leave Green Bay for the next part of their journey. They would travel south along the Fox River to their new home at Fort Winnebago.

This would be the last part of their trip. And it would be the hardest. They would no longer find villages or houses to sleep in. Instead, they would be camping outdoors.

Before they left, Mrs. Doty packed a basket of food for them that included ham and tongue, biscuits and plum cake, crackers, bread, and boiled pork.

Boiled pork? Juliette's East Coast manners had taught her that it was never proper for a lady to eat boiled pork, "even if starving in the woods." But without farms, stores, or kitchens on the frontier, there were few choices about what they could eat. Maybe boiled pork would be tasty when camping outdoors! Juliette was learning that life in the wilderness was very different from what she knew back home. She may have wondered if the old rules she learned in Connecticut would still make sense in this western frontier.

The steamboat was too big to travel on the Fox River. So Juliette and John switched to a smaller vessel called a Mackinaw boat. Mackinaw boats were popular with fur traders and other settlers for traveling on small rivers and lakes. They had flat bottoms, and their design was based on Indian canoes.

The Mackinaw boat was too small to hold all of Juliette's furniture and belongings. So they loaded the furniture onto a second boat, which would follow them down the river a few days later.

Juliette and John needed help with the small boat. An officer from Fort Winnebago named Captain Harney came to help them navigate the river. So did 3 French-Canadian **voyageurs**. The voyageurs' job was to steer the boat, cut wood for the campfires, and prepare meals at the campsites. These were just a few of the skills needed for survival on the frontier.

Voyageurs were hired to help paddle the canoe and set up camp.

They traveled up the Fox River. At the end of the first day, the voyageurs spotted the perfect location to set up camp. Camping in the wilderness! This was the first time Juliette would be sleeping outdoors, surrounded by nature. She could hardly wait.

voyageur: voi uh **zhur**

The voyageurs steered the boat toward the shore. But Juliette's excitement was too strong. She jumped out of the boat before it reached the land.

Splash!

The men pulled her out of the water and helped her to the shore. Juliette shook off the water and took a closer look around her. It was beautiful! She wanted to find a comfortable spot to sit and draw a picture before the sun set.

In Juliette's day, there were no cameras. People drew pictures to show others what they had seen. Juliette drew a picture of their small boat on the river and the men in their red hats and belts. She drew 2 tents on the shore and smoke rising from the campfire. In the distance, she drew a small waterfall at the edge of the forest.

For several days, Juliette, John, and the others traveled down the river. Each night they found a new place to camp, and the voyageurs would cut down a tree to make a fire. The fire was important to the group's survival. They used it to

WHI IMAGE ID 1943

Juliette drew this picture of a small camp along the Fox River. You can find this drawing in *Wau-Bun*.

cook breakfast and dinner and to prepare enough food for the next day's travel. When their clothes were wet, they would dry the clothes by the fire as well.

They slept in simple tents made of heavy canvas. Juliette learned how to create her own bed in the woods. First, she would gather armfuls of dry grass and spread it on the floor of her tent. Over that she would place a bearskin to keep her dry and warm. Then she would lie down and cover herself with blankets.

41

As they traveled up the river, they entered a beautiful lake called **Buttes des Morts**. Fields of wild rice grew along the lakeshore. Wild rice was a **staple** of the Indians' diet. Indian women would gather the rice in the early fall. They would store the rice and eat it throughout the winter.

Juliette watched Indian women in canoes gliding along the shore. She wrote: "They would push their canoes into the thick masses of the rice, bend it forward over the side with their paddles, and then beat the ripe **husks** off the stalks into a cloth spread in the canoe. After this, it is rubbed to separate the grain from the husk, and fanned in the open air. It is then put in their... bags and packed away for winter use.... The Indians are fond of it in the form of soup, with the addition of birds or **venison**."

Indian women gathered wild rice by bending it with their paddles, just as Juliette observed.

Buttes des Morts: byoo tuh mor   **staple:** something that is used widely and often   **husk:** the outer covering of a fruit or seed   **venison:** the meat of a deer used for food

They continued traveling down the river. Juliette noticed rushes growing at the water's edge. Rushes are plants that look like long grass. Juliette watched as the Indian women used the rushes to weave large mats. The mats would be used to help protect their homes from rain and wind.

Wild rice is still harvested and enjoyed in Wisconsin today.

Juliette wrote down what she saw: The women would sit on the ground with the rushes laid next to them. They would make thread from tree bark and a needle from bone. Carefully, they would use the needle to sew the rushes together so they formed a mat that was 5 or 6 feet long.

Throughout the trip, Juliette was amazed by the beautiful scenes that surrounded her. **Magnificent** trees stood along the river. Now and then she saw deer darting by, or a pair of cranes taking off in flight. The woods were filled with the colors of native wildflowers in pink, yellow, and purple.

Finally, their long journey was almost over. Juliette was so excited! But then they hit a difficult spot in the river. The

The Fox River

magnificent (mag **nif** uh suhnt): very beautiful or impressive

water became shallow. The river was tangled with wild rice plants. The voyagers struggled to row through the thick plants, and Juliette grew worried. It seemed like they would never arrive.

Juliette's drawing of Fort Winnebago. On the left of the river is the Indian Agency House, built for Juliette and John after they arrived. On the right of the river is the fort itself. This was one of many drawings that appeared in Juliette's book, *Wau-Bun.*

Suddenly, they looked up and saw the white walls of Fort Winnebago up ahead. The fort sat on a hill, overlooking the Fox River. The little boat continued the rest of its slow, winding trip up the river. They were almost home.

5

Arrival at Fort Winnebago

As their boat approached Fort Winnebago, Juliette heard a cheer from the shore. A crowd of people waited for them. Juliette and John stepped off the boat. They were greeted by the fort's commander, Major Twiggs, and his wife, Mrs. Twiggs.

Juliette and John had been promised a new home at the fort. But when they arrived, the home had not been built. Major Twiggs invited Juliette and John to live with them until the rest of their furniture arrived.

Mrs. Twiggs prepared 2 rooms for Juliette and John. She wanted the Kinzies to feel comfortable in their new surroundings.

And what surroundings they were!

WHI IMAGE ID 28343

Fort Winnebago

The fort consisted of neat wooden buildings and a tall flagpole. The fort sat on high ground between the Fox River and the Wisconsin River. In front of the fort was a meadow with a well-worn path running through it. The path was 2 miles long. It was called the **portage**.

COURTESY OF THE LIBRARY OF CONGRESS, CAI - ROGERS, NO. 72

The portage allowed travelers to carry their boats between the Fox River and the Wisconsin River. The portage helped connect the Great Lakes with the Mississippi River.

Travelers portaging a canoe

portage: por tij

47

Juliette admired the view from the fort. The woods were bright with fall color. Many Ho-Chunk and Menominee Indians were coming to the fort to receive their **annual** payment of silver before the winter. Indian lodges were scattered around the fort. Farther down, Juliette saw the white tents of traders who had come to provide winter supplies to the Indians in the region.

The Indians and other settlers were eager to meet Juliette. And Juliette was excited to meet her new neighbors. She looked forward to sharing her eastern education and refined ways with the Indians and settlers.

But Juliette's own education was just beginning. In Juliette's time, many non-Indian people believed Indians were not as smart or educated because they did not have the same schools or customs that were found in non-Indian communities. But Juliette soon learned that Indian communities had valuable customs and knowledge of their own to share.

Juliette learned from every person she met, Indians and settlers alike. She paid attention to the way they dressed, the

annual: happening once a year

way they talked, what they thought, and how they acted. She was curious about their relationships with other people and the land. She was a good observer. She knew her stories of life on the frontier would someday be important.

Juliette spent her first day at Fort Winnebago meeting the chiefs and elders from the Indian community. She met the leader of the Ho-Chunk, whose name was **Kar-ray-mau-nee**, or Walking Rain. She met the leader Old **Day-kau-ray** and the distinguished **Hoo-wau-nee-kah**, or Little Elk. And she met White Crow, known as **Kau-ray-kaw-saw-kaw**, who led the Rock River Indians.

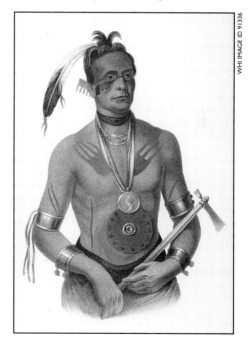

Juliette was eager to meet the Ho-Chunk women. A few days after she arrived, a group of Ho-Chunk women came to visit. They laid down their blankets and sat on the floor

WHI IMAGE ID 91336

Ho-Chunk leader Little Elk

Kar-ray-mau-nee: kahr ruh **maw** nee   **Day-kau-ray:** day **kaw** ruh   **Hoo-wau-nee-kah:** hoo **waw** nee kuh
Kau-ray-kaw-saw-kaw: kaw ruh **kaw** saw kaw

in a circle. Juliette offered the
women a plate of pastries. The
first woman took the plate
from Juliette and poured all
the pastries onto her blanket!
Juliette was surprised by the

woman's appetite, but she wanted to make sure everyone else
had something to eat.

Juliette prepared a second plate of pastries. This time she
held onto the plate as she offered a pastry to the next woman.
The next woman scooped all the pastries off the plate and into
her own blanket.

Juliette was **astonished**. She had run out of pastries for
the others. What would she do? She sat down to think about
it. Then she noticed the 2 women were quietly dividing the
pastries among the other women so that everyone had an equal
share.

Juliette realized she had misunderstood the women's
actions. When she understood why they were taking all the

astonished (uh **ston** isht): struck with sudden wonder or surprise

50

pastries, she was impressed. Whenever food was offered, each person would gather enough for the entire group. They would wait until the food was equally shared with everyone before eating.

The second boat with Juliette's furniture arrived several days later. As the men lifted the boxes off the boat, water poured out of every corner. Every piece of furniture was soaked, but Juliette was not **discouraged**.

"There is nothing to do but to be patient and make of the best of it," Juliette said.

Juliette and John settled into their new life. Living at the fort meant they had to live by military **routines**. Instead of an alarm clock, a **bugler** would announce each part of the day

with a special bugle call: wake-up (called **reveille**), meal times, and bedtime (called retreat).

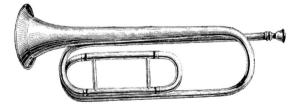

---

discouraged (dis **kur** ijd): made to feel less determined, hopeful, or confident **routine** (roo **teen**): a usual order and way of doing something **bugler**: **byoo** glur **reveille**: **rev** uh lee

Life at the fort required the **cooperation** of many people. There were no towns or shopping malls, so the residents had to work together to make sure they had what they needed to survive. The soldiers at the fort had many duties. They protected the fort, harvested trees for lumber, gathered stones for construction, tended vegetable gardens, and hunted wild animals for food.

One of the buildings at Fort Winnebago was a hospital. How does this building compare to hospitals today?

The fort was the center of activity for the settlers who lived nearby. The fort housed a hospital, icehouse, bathhouse, laundry,

cooperation (koh op uh **ray** suhn): the act of working together to get something done

and a store called a **commissary**, where food, equipment, and supplies were sold. The Indian Agent, blacksmith, interpreters, and guides were part of the fort community. They lived in homes near the fort.

The fort served a role with the Indians, as well. The Indians might travel to the fort several times a year to receive their payments of silver and supplies. While they were there, they could purchase items such as pots, beads, guns, and tools from the local traders.

The Indians also came to the fort to meet with the Indian Agent. They shared news and stories about their tribes, requested food and supplies, and discussed government **policies**. Often John Kinzie would help them settle tribal disputes and disagreements with local settlers. Because John Kinzie represented the US government, the Indians would come to him with concerns and questions about how the government was treating them. The Indians might camp outside the fort for a short time. When they were finished with their business, the Indians would return home.

commissary: **kom** uh ser ee   policy: a set of guidelines or rules that determine how something is done

In the evenings, Juliette entertained herself with books, music, and drawing. But she missed the social gatherings of her earlier days. The men at the fort built a small theater. Juliette was soon directing the soldiers in weekly theater performances and musicals. It was fun for people to come together and enjoy themselves in such a remote place!

The days passed quickly, and Juliette was happy with life at the fort. However, a gloom soon spread over that happiness. A messenger from Chicago arrived with horrible news. Juliette's favorite uncle, Dr. Wolcott, was very ill in Chicago. Juliette wanted to go see him, but it was a difficult trip for someone unfamiliar with the land. Instead, John left right away and rode to Chicago on horseback to be by Dr. Wolcott's side. Several days later Juliette's uncle died. Juliette was **heartbroken**.

When John returned to Fort Winnebago, he made Juliette a promise. They would travel to Chicago together in the spring to visit John's family. Juliette looked forward to the trip. She **eagerly** began planning during the rest of the long, dark winter.

heartbroken: overcome by sorrow   **eagerly** (ee gur lee): very excitedly and with interest

54

6

Life among the Ho-Chunk

The government promised to build Juliette and John a comfortable new house when they arrived, but the house was still not ready. While they waited, Juliette and John moved into a simple log home built for the fort's blacksmith.

Juliette and John's log home might have looked like this one.

Juliette made the best of what she had. She spread Indian mats across the floor, placed her piano and other furniture around the room, and hung pictures on the walls.

The log home was located on the prairie, across the river from the fort. It was an ideal place to visit with people as they made their way to and from the fort.

WHI IMAGE ID 89549

Ho-Chunk Indians gathered in a long structure called a ciproke. They would display their goods on the long blanket in the middle of the floor for trade with settlers.

Juliette began to learn about the everyday lives of the Indians. She wrote about how the Indians looked, how they treated each other, and what they believed. They taught her about their beliefs and ways of life. Juliette wrote down what she saw and the stories she was told.

Stories were an important way the Ho-Chunk shared their culture. The head of each household shared history and information about their tribal clan with the other members of the family. This history was told in stories or song.

Some tribes had an official storyteller who would go from village to village telling stories. Some of these stories taught Indian listeners about their own history and customs. Listening to these stories helped Juliette begin to understand the lives of the Ho-Chunk people.

Juliette was not the only one interested in learning about others. The Indian women were interested in Juliette and her ways of life, too. They would visit and look at Juliette's strange belongings. They would laugh with delight at the different objects in Juliette's house and her eastern ways of cooking, cleaning, and reading.

Juliette learned that gift giving was an important form of communication and respect between Indians and settlers. The Indian women would bring Juliette gifts of venison, ducks, pigeons, berries, wild plums, and cranberries. They would bring her beautiful mats for the floor and table, wooden bowls and ladles, and deerskin or porcupine quills.

One of Juliette's favorite visitors was a young woman named Elizabeth. Elizabeth was the daughter of the Ho-Chunk leader Day-kau-ray. Elizabeth suffered from an illness that made her sore. Juliette saw that Elizabeth was in pain. Juliette offered her new friend a remedy that made her feel better. Elizabeth was very grateful to Juliette for her help.

Juliette's pet, Fan, probably looked a lot like like this fawn!

One day, Elizabeth arrived with a thank-you present for Juliette. It was a young **fawn**. The creature had soft eyes and a spotted coat. Juliette did not

fawn: a young deer

58

know how she would take care of a wild animal in her home. To her surprise, the fawn followed her like a pet dog. Juliette named it Fan. Wherever Juliette went, Fan would go, too. At breakfast, Fan would lie under the table at Juliette's feet.

One day Juliette heard rattling in the kitchen. She ran to see what was making all the noise. Fan had climbed onto a shelf, looking for a place to lie down among the dishes. Juliette realized Fan needed a cozy place in which to rest. Every morning when it was time for Fan to take her nap, Juliette would open a large green umbrella and set it up in the corner. Fan would curl up underneath it and fall fast asleep.

Juliette soon learned that Indian dances were part of their gift-giving culture, too. Unlike the social dances of Juliette's childhood, Indian dances were often used for important **ceremonies**. Sometimes the dances honored tribal members or marked important times of the year. Dance was also a formal way for the Indians to show their thanks. After John gave the Indians their silver payment, the Indians would perform a dance of thanks.

ceremony (**ser** uh moh nee): an act performed according to fixed rules especially as part of a social or religious event

Here Ho-Chunk dancers perform the Eagle Dance. In her time, Juliette might have seen this dance performed, too.

Juliette saw many types of dances. The male dancers would paint their faces with tribal patterns and wear a **headdress** or ornaments in their hair. These ornaments might include feathers from eagles, wild turkeys, or roosters. Sometimes they would even pluck feathers from Juliette's chickens for their beautiful outfits!

headdress (**hed** dres): a covering or ornament for the head

The men would arrange themselves in a circle. They danced to the music of a drum and a rattle, which was often made of dried hide, bone, and stones. The Ho-Chunk women would stand aside and sing. On special occasions, the women would form their own circle and dance together in perfect **rhythm**.

After the dance was finished, Juliette and John would place presents in the center of the circle. The dancers divided the gifts equally among themselves. Once thanks had been given and gifts exchanged, it was time to go home.

Some modern-day historians believe that before Juliette came to Fort Winnebago, she planned to teach the Indians how to read English and live

HISTORIC INDIAN AGENCY HOUSE

Today, Ho-Chunk members perform traditional dances at the Historic Indian Agency House.

rhythm (riTH uhm): a regular repeated pattern of beats, sounds, activity, or movements

like people in Connecticut. Juliette originally believed that people living on the frontier would want to have the same education and comforts she had enjoyed back home.

But after meeting and living with the Indians, Juliette changed her mind. She realized that different cultures defined happiness and success in different ways.

She tried to see herself through their eyes. She thought the Indians might say to each other: "Look at [the white people] . . . always **toiling** and striving—always wearing a brow of care—shut up in houses—afraid of wind and the rain—suffering when they are **deprived** of the comforts of life! We, on the contrary, live a life of freedom and happiness. We hunt and fish, and pass our time pleasantly in the open woods and prairies. If we are hungry we take some game; or if we do not find that, we can go without. . . . What should we gain by changing ourselves into white men?"

As Juliette got to know the Ho-Chunk, she developed a deep respect for their beliefs and ways of life, even if they were different from her own. She often heard the Ho-Chunk

toiling: working hard and long   **deprived** (di **prɪvd**): kept from having something people explain: "If the Great Spirit had wished [us] different from what [we] are, he would have made [us] so." She now understood how to respect the differences between her culture and that of the Indians.

But she did not realize how these differences would lead to a major turning point in history.

7

Traveling to Chicago

Juliette's first winter in Wisconsin was cold and snowy. The walls of the Kinzies' log cabin were **drafty**. Juliette and John stuffed the cracks in the walls with cotton and covered them with strips of paper to keep out the cold. They lit a fire in the fireplace to keep the rooms warm. But it was still so cold that pitchers of water froze to solid ice.

Finally, March arrived. The snow began to melt, and spring was on its way. Juliette remembered John's promise to visit Chicago. With the weather so warm, Juliette was sure they could make the journey without any problems.

They began to prepare for the trip. They would ride to Chicago

drafty: having unusually cool air moving through

on horseback. With no stores on the frontier, Juliette had to make her own special traveling clothes. Luckily, the fort's cook knew how to sew. Together, Juliette and the cook designed a riding outfit, with a long dress, a cloak, a straw bonnet, and gloves. She would carry a hunting knife in a small pouch around her neck and a tin cup around her saddle bow.

Juliette packed food for the trip: biscuits, meat, coffee, and sugar. The food was stored in large bags and loaded onto the horse. Finally, they were ready to begin their journey.

The distance between Fort Winnebago and Chicago was less than 180 miles. Juliette and John would need to travel across grasslands, forests, marshes, lakes, and rivers. They thought their journey would take 6 days. Today, the same trip would take only a few hours.

Juliette and John left Fort Winnebago on a warm spring morning in March. They were joined by 2 guides named **Plante** and **Pierre** Roy, who would help them find their way.

Plante: plahnt **Pierre**: pee er

Juliette was in high spirits. She had never traveled by horseback before. But she was eager to learn. With her bonnet, gloves, and **fashionable** traveling clothes, she felt ready for an easy trip across the prairie. She laughed at John's suggestion to wear warm socks, a wool hat, and a scarf to keep her warm.

The day started out sunny. But by the afternoon, the weather turned cold and raw. The wind lifted Juliette's hat. Her hands became stiff and swollen from the cold.

The travelers soon arrived at a stream near a place the settlers called the Four Lakes, near present-day Madison, Wisconsin. They found an opening in the woods and decided to set up camp for the night.

It was windy and cold, so the men hurried to set up the tents and build a campfire. Juliette changed into dry clothes while the men cooked a ham over the fire.

The meal was not fancy. They did not have tables, chairs, or dishes. Instead, they only had what they could carry on

fashionable: following current fashion or style

WHI IMAGE ID 3776

Travelers rest for the night around a campfire.

horseback: "a coffeepot, a teakettle, and each rider his own tin cup and hunting-knife."

Eating dinner on the prairie was a different experience from the meals at home. First, Juliette drew her knife from its pouch, wiped it on a napkin, and used it to stir her coffee. Then she used the knife to cut a piece of ham. She placed the ham on a biscuit, which served as her plate. After dinner, she cleaned her knife with prairie grass. This was certainly not the way she had been taught to dine back home.

Juliette used a tin cup that looked a lot like this one.

The next morning, Juliette and the rest of the traveling party packed up camp. As they rode away, they passed a small Ho-Chunk village on the shore of the Four Lakes. The camp looked beautiful in the morning sun. Blue smoke curled from the tops of the lodges. The trees and bushes were covered with a light snow that had fallen during the night. The lake shone and sparkled. The Indians and travelers shouted out greetings to each other as they passed.

They rode toward their next stop, a place called Morrison's Cabin near hills called the Blue Mounds.

Only a handful of non-Indian settlers lived on the frontier. They lived in rustic log cabins they built in the wilderness. There were no hotels. Instead, settlers would invite travelers to stay in their homes. Life on the frontier was often lonely, and the settlers enjoyed having visitors, even if they were strangers. The settlers would ask visitors to share the news and fashions of the outside world.

Inside a frontier cabin

The route to Blue Mounds was a small, simple trail over rolling prairie. Snow had collected in the hollows. Riding was difficult, and the horses struggled over the soggy trail.

When they finally reached the Blue Mounds, Juliette learned that Morrison's Cabin was still 7 miles away. She was so cold and tired that she cried out in despair. But the riders and their horses marched on.

When they finally rode up to Morrison's Cabin, Juliette was freezing, sore, and exhausted. "This will never do!" John said. "Tomorrow we will turn around and return to Fort Winnebago."

Before Juliette could respond, the door to the small log house opened. Mrs. Morrison invited them inside.

Juliette changed her riding clothes and drank warm tea. Soon she felt better. She joined the others for a party of good food and conversation.

Mrs. Morrison was a kind and cheerful woman. She had once lived in Connecticut, too. She and Juliette had friends in common. Juliette was happy to share what news she had, but she was more interested in learning how Mrs. Morrison lived.

Mrs. Morrison told Juliette about her lonely days on the frontier, where the only company was her husband and 2 servants. It had been more than a year since she had seen another female settler. The 2 women spent the evening talking about old friends and telling stories. In such a remote place, it was nice to share memories of home.

The next morning, Juliette felt better. She and John decided not to return to Fort Winnebago after all. Instead, they left for their next stop, a small cabin called Hamilton's Diggings.

The trail to Hamilton's Diggings was hard to find. The rolling prairie stretched out for miles, with no sign of anyone to help them. The weather became colder, and the wind was sharp and piercing. Prairie wolves watched them from afar.

They traveled on, noticing long openings in the ground. These openings were called diggings. The diggings looked like big graves. They marked the areas where explorers had searched for a mineral called **galena**. Galena contained lead, an important element for making many useful items. Explorers were eager to find this valuable resource.

galena: guh **lee** nuh

71

Lead Mining in Southwestern Wisconsin

The Northwest Territory had many resources. But none was more important in the early 1800s than galena ore. This shiny gray mineral was found in the southwestern corner of what later became Wisconsin. Galena was an important mineral source of lead. It attracted a rush of settlers to the area. They mined the galena ore and smelted it down in hot furnaces to extract the lead.

Lead was used to make many items, such as pipes, weights, **ammunition**, and paint.

One of the many lead mines in Wisconsin

The Indians had collected the galena ore for thousands of years. When the settlers arrived, they began collecting galena, too. The settlers quickly set up mining operations to extract the mineral from the land. The mining operations were called diggings. Some miners simply burrowed into the land, which earned them the nickname "badgers."

Lead mining was rough and dirty work. But it attracted thousands of new settlers to the area, looking to strike it rich.

ammunition (am yuh **nish** uhn): objects fired from weapons

72

Finally, Juliette, John, and the guides came upon the log cabins of Hamilton's Diggings.

They climbed off their horses and hurried inside. A large fire burned in the fireplace, and the room was warm.

Their host, William "Billy" Hamilton, came in to greet them. He was the son of Alexander Hamilton, one of the founding fathers of the United States. Like Juliette, Billy had left his family out East and moved to the frontier. He became a lead miner and set up Hamilton's Diggings so he and his workers could mine valuable lead from the countryside.

WHI IMAGE ID 3458

William "Billy" Hamilton, in his finery

Billy was ragged and unshaven, but he was happy to welcome Juliette and John for dinner.

A crew of miners sat at the long dinner table with them. The miners were the roughest looking people Juliette had ever seen! Even though she felt uncomfortable among people so different from herself, Juliette enjoyed the warmth and shelter.

For the next few days, Juliette, John, and their guides traveled on, staying in other settlers' cabins along the way. After a certain point, however, there were no more cabins until they reached Chicago. For the rest of the trip, they would need to camp outdoors. They could use only the food and supplies they carried with them.

Instead of roads, they followed Indian trails across the countryside. They had to rely on directions from people they met along the way. They were told to find the Sauk Indian trail to Chicago. They were warned that if they missed the trail, they might get lost in the Winnebago swamp and never find their way out.

The trails were hard to find. The directions were confusing. John and the guides argued about which way to go. A blinding snowstorm made it difficult for them to find their way.

Juliette was worried. The trip was taking much longer than they had planned. They were lost and cold. And they were down to their last 3 biscuits. After that, there would be no more food.

The gloomy team continued on, not sure where they were headed. They followed a trail that led eastward, but the trail ended at a wide, rushing river. John noticed an empty camp with Indian wigwams on the other side of the river. Unless they could cross the river and use the camp for shelter, they would surely die.

The river was lined with jagged ice. There was no way for them to cross the river on horseback.

Juliette was discouraged, but she tried to keep a brave face. The weather was getting colder, and the skies were getting darker. They shouted for help. It was their last hope.

Suddenly, Juliette's horse began to prance and jump. The horse knew someone was nearby!

A dog ran out from under the bushes  and began to bark at them. They followed the dog into the woods and found an Indian woman and young girl digging roots for food. The woman and girl seemed frightened by the traveling party. But when John addressed them in their own Potawatomi language, they smiled.

They agreed to help Juliette, John, and the guides cross the river. First, they helped Juliette across the river in their small canoe. The young girl stayed with Juliette on the banks of the river. The older woman returned to the other side to pick up the men and their supplies.

Juliette waited for the canoe to return. She sat on a tree trunk and looked out across the dark waters. She thought about how dangerous the trip had become. Had they arrived even moments later, they would have missed meeting the

Indians and could not have crossed the river. Juliette knew that without the women's help, they would have starved and frozen in the wilderness.

Juliette had been brave and cheerful the entire trip. But this time, she broke down and cried.

After a moment, she asked herself: "What would my friends in the East think if they could see me now?" She remembered the people who had warned that her plans for adventure were a bad idea. They said the frontier was no place for a lady.

These thoughts made Juliette dry her tears and stand tall. She did not travel all this way to feel sorry for herself. She would show those folks out East that a young woman could survive and enjoy life on the frontier!

The Indian woman led the weary travelers to her lodge and invited them inside. It was Juliette's first chance to see the inside of an Indian home. The lodge was nicely arranged. Four sticks of wood formed a square in the center of the floor. Inside that square was a campfire, with the smoke escaping through a hole in the roof. The lodge was constructed of neat mats. Dried food and household goods hung from bags on the walls.

Hanging over the fire was a large kettle. The woman served Juliette a dish of potatoes from the kettle. The woman encouraged the travelers to set up their tents nearby and camp for the night. Juliette was grateful for the food and the woman's kindness. She knew the woman had saved their lives.

That night a violent snowstorm hit the area. Sounds like gunfire echoed through the woods as giant trees cracked under the weight of the snow.

The next morning they surveyed the damage. Nearly 50 trees had fallen around them. The Indian woman's husband guided them through the fallen trees to their next destination. The storm made the travel worse, but they continued on their way.

They continued for several more days. One morning they looked across the prairie and saw 2 trees standing along the horizon. John smiled and pointed at the trees. He had planted them when he was boy. Now they had grown tall and were landmarks to anyone traveling to Chicago.

The trees meant they were only 12 miles away.

When they finally reached Chicago, they were warmly welcomed by John's family. Juliette was relieved to finish such a difficult journey. Though the trip should have taken just 6 days, the dangerous journey took them nearly 2 weeks!

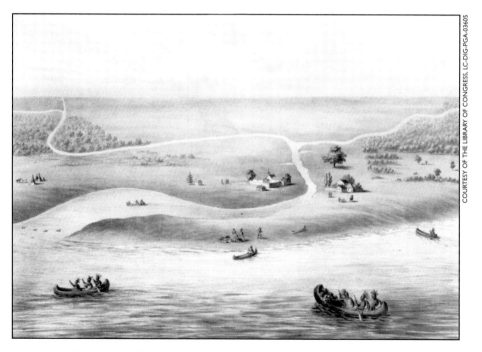

COURTESY OF THE LIBRARY OF CONGRESS, LC-DIG-PGA-03605

A view of Chicago in 1820. John lived here before he and Juliette married and moved to Fort Winnebago.

8

A Family Visit

Today, Chicago is a big city of almost 3 million people.
When Juliette arrived, it was a small village of cabins and
buildings on swampy land. Fort Dearborn stood across the
Chicago River at the edge of Lake Michigan. John's family had
been some of the first non-Indian settlers in the area. They
knew much about its history and traditions.

The Kinzies' home sat across from Fort Dearborn, on
the northern bank of the river. The house was a long, low
building with a porch extending along its front. Nice trees
and a fine garden surrounded the home. There were several
small buildings behind the house, including a dairy, bake
house, and stables. It was the nicest house in the area.

Juliette drew this picture of the Kinzie family home.

Juliette was excited to meet John's family. They spent several days talking and getting to know each other. The Kinzie women entertained Juliette with stories about their family and their adventures. They described their early days in Chicago and the struggles of life on the frontier. And they told her funny stories about settlers and visitors. Once, a complete stranger entered their home, slept in one of their beds, and ate their food. When he was ready to leave, he asked how much he owed them. They all laughed. The stranger had mistaken their house for a hotel!

81

WHI IMAGE ID 28328

In the early 1800s, Chicago was a small settlement. Here you can see Fort Dearborn in the center and the Kinzie family's home on the right.

John's mother knew that someday stories about life on the frontier would help other people learn about the area's history. She told Juliette: "Write these things down, as I tell them to you. Hereafter our children and even strangers will be interested in hearing the story of our early lives ..." Juliette listened to her mother-in-law and understood. She, too, had experiences and stories to share.

Juliette and John stayed in Chicago for more than 2 months. Then it was time to return to Fort Winnebago. John's mother and sister and several other relatives joined them on the trip back to Fort Winnebago. The weather was much nicer for travel, and they followed a different route home.

They traveled across gently swelling hills, lovely valleys, and bright sparkling streams. Juliette saw delightful birds and wildlife along the way.

They traveled through an Indian village called Maunk-suck, now known as Lake Geneva, Wisconsin, settled around a

WHI IMAGE ID109891

Juliette drew this image of a sparking lake, lush forest, and a small encampment called Big Foot's Village or Maunk-suck. Today, this is known as Lake Geneva, Wisconsin.

beautiful lake. Juliette and her family were the first non-Indians to see the area. Juliette marveled at the lake's beauty and the kindness of the Indian people who lived there.

They continued traveling northward, past Lake **Koshkonong** and through beautiful prairies. After several days, they arrived back home to the familiar sight of Fort Winnebago.

Koshkonong: kahsh kuh nahng

9

News of Trouble: The Black Hawk War

In the summer of 1831, Juliette and John finally received approval from the government to build a new Indian Agency House. Unlike their rough log cabin, the Agency House would be a fine home, with large rooms and sturdy walls. Workmen brought **expensive** construction materials from Green Bay and Saint Louis. It was going to be a grand home!

Juliette was pregnant with her first child. She looked forward to settling into the new house to enjoy a time of peace and happiness.

The Indian Agency House, shown in a 1932 photograph, 100 years after it was built

expensive (ek **spen** siv): costly

An example of a treaty document between the US government and Indian tribes

But change was coming. Juliette and John received upsetting news from the Ho-Chunk leader White Crow and other chiefs of the Rock River Indians. The Sauk leader Black Hawk was unhappy with a treaty that had been signed by the US government. Black Hawk was crossing the Mississippi River with his tribe to take back his people's land from the white settlers. There was tension between the US government and the Indians. Everyone worried there would be war.

But this trouble wasn't new. It had started many years earlier.

In 1804, the US government signed a treaty with Indian nations across what is today Illinois, Iowa, and

Wisconsin. The treaty made the Indians promise to someday leave these lands in exchange for annual payments of silver.

By the 1820s, more non-Indian people were moving into the area to settle. The land was rich with lead, and the settlers were interested in mining it. The government wanted room for the settlers to move in. So government officials ordered the Sauk Indians to leave their homelands in Illinois and move west of the Mississippi River. They made the Sauk Indians leave before they could harvest their crops. Government officials promised they would deliver plenty of corn so the Sauk families would have food to eat in the winter.

PORTRAIT OF BLACK HAWK, GEORGE CATLIN, ARTIST. SMITHSONIAN AMERICAN ART MUSEUM

When Black Hawk and his people moved west, they discovered their new land was poorly suited for growing crops. The corn never arrived. Black Hawk's people began to suffer from hunger.

Black Hawk, a leader of the Sauk tribe

Black Hawk and his people were angry. They believed the treaty was unfair. During the winter of 1831, they returned to their old homes in Illinois to harvest their crops. But settlers had already moved in and were harvesting the fields themselves.

WHI IMAGE ID 27177

Militia members fighting Black Hawk and his people often wore uniforms like this one.

The settlers were afraid that Black Hawk and his people would attack them. They asked the Illinois **militia** to guard them.

Black Hawk saw the militia. He knew his people were outnumbered. So he sent in some of his men with white flags to surrender. However, the militia men misunderstood their wish for a peaceful surrender. The militia men panicked and fired their rifles, killing several of Black Hawk's people. The Sauk fired

militia (muh **li** shuh): a group of citizens with military training who are called into service in emergencies

back in self-defense. This started what is now called the Black Hawk War.

Black Hawk realized he could not win a battle against the US militia. He tried to lead his people back across the Mississippi River, but the militia blocked his way. Black Hawk decided to cross the river farther north, so he and his followers headed up the Rock River into what is now Wisconsin.

Traveling with the hungry Sauk families was slow. Black Hawk raided the settlers' farms to get food for his starving people. The settlers were angry and afraid. As Black Hawk and his followers moved north, several battles broke out. People worried the Sauk Indians might attack places like Fort Winnebago.

Juliette worried about what this news meant for the safety and friendships between the settlers and their Indian neighbors.

She was right to be concerned. People at Fort Winnebago heard the US Army was pursuing Black Hawk and the Sauk Indians.

Juliette thought she knew why there was going to be trouble. She knew the US government had gradually taken away the Indians' broad and beautiful lands. She believed the only thing the Indians had received in return was "a few thousand dollars in silver and presents, along with settlers who treated them poorly."

As the Indian Agent, it was John's job to talk with the Indians. John held a meeting with the Ho-Chunk chiefs. The chiefs promised to do their best to keep the Ho-Chunk out of the war. But they could not guarantee that the other Indian tribes would be so peaceful.

Fear and tension grew in the fort community. There were rumors that Indians were coming to the fort to kill the residents. The soldiers chopped down trees to make a tall fence to protect the fort from any attack. Juliette and her family left their home each night and slept inside the fort for protection. The officers also made a rule that no Indians could come into the fort area. Sadly, Juliette was separated from her Ho-Chunk and Menominee visitors.

Finally, the danger of war at the fort was too much. John stayed at Fort Winnebago, but Juliette and their family boarded a boat and traveled to the safety of Fort Howard. The trip was dangerous. Rumors of Indians sneaking up on them made the travelers nervous. A deadly **cholera epidemic** was making its way toward Green Bay. The travelers were frightened by warring Indians on one side and deadly disease on the other. They worried there was no safe place to go.

Meanwhile, Black Hawk and his people traveled northwest toward the Wisconsin River. If they could reach the Wisconsin River, they could follow it west to the Mississippi River. Then they could find safety on the other side.

However, the US Army and militia were closing in on Black Hawk and his people. The Battle of Wisconsin Heights took place on the banks of the Wisconsin River, near present-day Sauk City, Wisconsin. Black Hawk's warriors fought to protect the Sauk people as they tried to cross the Wisconsin River. Many survived this battle but later died from starvation as they continued fleeing west.

cholera: **kol** ur uh   epidemic (ep uh **dem** ik): a rapidly spreading outbreak of disease

WHI IMAGE ID 2286

A painting of the Wisconsin Heights Battlefield, the site of an important battle in the Black Hawk War

The final battle occurred when the Sauk Indians were about to reach safety across the Mississippi River at the mouth of the Bad Axe River. Once again, the Indians tried to surrender, but the Army ignored their **pleas**. In the **massacre** that followed, many Indian women, children, older people, and warriors were killed. Of Black Hawk's original 1,200

plea: an earnest appeal   **massacre** (**mas** uh kur): the violent and cruel killing of a large number of people

WHI IMAGE ID 2466

The battle of Bad Axe, August 2, 1832

followers, only 150 to 200 survived. Black Hawk and the small group of survivors tried to escape to safety. Eventually they surrendered and were imprisoned.

By August 1832, Juliette and her family returned to Fort Winnebago. The war had ended. But the challenges were far from over.

The Future Presidents: Lincoln and Davis

Juliette wrote about her experiences on the frontier and how they shaped her life. Would it surprise you to know that similar experiences also shaped the lives of 2 future presidents?

In 1832, Jefferson Davis was a young **lieutenant**. He served in the US military at Fort Winnebago and at Fort Crawford, down the river at **Prairie du Chien**. At the end of the Black Hawk War, Davis was responsible for escorting the captured Black Hawk to prison.

Farther south in Illinois, a young Abraham Lincoln answered the governor's call to capture Black Hawk. Lincoln served as a captain in the Illinois militia. Lincoln travelled with other soldiers and followed Black Hawk's trail into Wisconsin before turning back into Illinois. This was Lincoln's first military experience. Some people believe his military service helped pave the way for him to become president.

Abraham Lincoln was elected president of the United States in 1860. Jefferson Davis was a senator from the Southern state of Mississippi. Lincoln and Davis disagreed on the issue of slavery. In 1861, Davis left the US Senate. He became the president of the newly formed Confederate States of America. The Union and the Confederate armies fought against one another in the Civil War.

lieutenant: loo **ten** uhnt   **Prairie du Chien**: **prayr** ee duh shayn

It is possible that Juliette knew Jefferson Davis from his time at Fort Winnebago. But did Juliette meet Abraham Lincoln during his time in the Northwest Territory? Probably not. But she did write him personal letters from her home in Chicago during the Civil War.

This is the earliest-known portrait of Abraham Lincoln. Abraham Lincoln served in the Illinois militia during the Black Hawk War. Almost 30 years later, he became the sixteenth president of the United States of America.

Jefferson Davis, a US senator and the president of the Confederate States of America

10

A Difficult Winter

The Black Hawk War was a tragic time for the Sauk, Ho-Chunk, and other Indian tribes in the region. Many of Black Hawk's followers were killed in the battles. Some drowned as they tried to cross the river. Others starved to death as they tried to survive on acorns, elm bark, and grass. The stories of their suffering left Juliette feeling sad and worried.

After the war, the US government made the Indians sign a treaty and give up all of their land south and east of the Wisconsin River. This was known as the Treaty of 1832. It was signed at Rock Island, Illinois. As a result of the treaty, the government planned to sell the Indians' land to non-Indian settlers. The treaty would change the lives of the Indians forever.

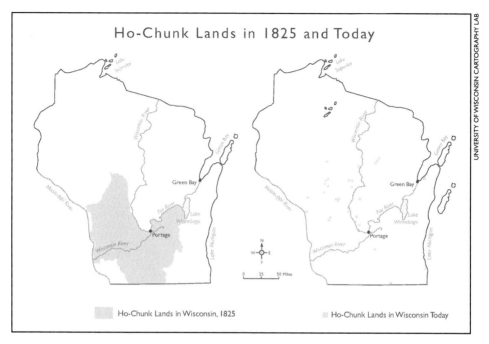

Ho-Chunk Lands in 1825 and Today

Ho-Chunk Lands in Wisconsin, 1825

Ho-Chunk Lands in Wisconsin Today

UNIVERSITY OF WISCONSIN CARTOGRAPHY LAB

The Ho-Chunk people were forced to leave many of their lands. Compare the Ho-Chunk's vast land in 1825 with their land today.

John Kinzie attended the treaty gathering. It was a large ceremony, attended by US government officials and leaders of local Indian tribes.

Because of the treaty, the Ho-Chunk families were forced to leave their homes and move north and westward. They needed food and supplies for the journey. After the ceremony, the Ho-Chunk people traveled to Fort Winnebago to wait for the arrival of their annual silver payment. They needed the money to buy food and supplies for the upcoming winter. However, the money was late in coming.

The Indians' food supply that autumn was scarce. The war and the new treaty had driven the Ho-Chunk away from their homes and gardens. They had little food for the winter other than a small amount of wild rice.

John worried the Ho-Chunk people might starve, so he asked a merchant in Green Bay to send 2 boatloads of corn. But by the time the corn was ready, winter had come. The Fox River had frozen over. There was no way to ship the corn down the river until the ice melted.

John told the Ho-Chunk to go to their hunting grounds to find food. He would contact them when the silver and corn arrived. In the winter, the Ho-Chunk people usually hunted animals by following their tracks across the snow. But the snow was very light that year. This made it difficult to track and hunt animals for food. Many of the wild animals had left the area during the Black Hawk War. It was getting more and more difficult to find anything to eat.

Back at the fort that November, construction of the new Indian Agency House was finally finished. But it was hard for Juliette to be happy in her new home.

The parlor of the Indian Agency House. Juliette had put her piano on a boat and shipped it to Fort Winnebago so she could enjoy music on the frontier.

Ho-Chunk visitors sometimes came to the Indian Agency House in need of food. Many Indians tried to stay alive with soup made from the slippery elm tree or stewed acorns. Several people died from starvation. Juliette shared some of her own food supply, but she did not have much extra to give.

One day a familiar face appeared at Juliette's window. It was her old friend Elizabeth. The girl looked tired and thin. Juliette took her own plate of food and gave it to Elizabeth, expecting her to eat the food all at once. But Elizabeth took the food, made signs she would return, and walked away. When she brought back the empty dish, Juliette was almost sure Elizabeth had given the food to others without taking any for herself.

Juliette was worried. It had been a long time since John had ordered the boatloads of corn. He wrote letters and sent messages trying to hurry the delivery, with no luck.

People were beginning to think the corn would never arrive. The situation was miserable and scary.

Finally, the ice melted. Boats were beginning to move down the river. A shout from the fort announced good news. Someone had seen the boats of corn on the horizon!

Hundreds of Indians gathered on the shore. The boats slowly made their way through the winding river toward the fort. The crowd watched nervously. Would there be enough to feed the starving people?

A cheer went up from the crowd as soon as the first boat reached the shore. They took their hatchets and opened barrel after barrel of corn. They filled their containers and began to prepare meals on nearby fires.

The Ho-Chunk families were relieved, and so were Juliette and John. They celebrated the arrival of the much-needed corn. But despite their happiness, this was the beginning of difficult times for the Ho-Chunk people. It had been a long and dangerous winter, and there would be hard times ahead. Once everyone had their share of food and supplies, they left to start the new season.

Troubled Times for the Ho-Chunk

The winter of 1832 was the beginning of troubled times for the Ho-Chunk people. The treaty of 1832 forced the Ho-Chunk to sell all of their land south and east of the Wisconsin River to the US government. This represented almost half of the Ho-Chunk's land. The remaining Ho-Chunk people would be forced to give up the rest of their land and leave in 1837.

The Ho-Chunk people were forced to move 5 times after they left Wisconsin: first to Iowa, then to 2 different places in Minnesota, then farther west to South Dakota, and finally to Nebraska.

The new locations had many problems. The soil was not good for growing food. Sometimes the new locations were next to warring tribes, and the Ho-Chunk were hurt by the warfare. The land they were forced to live on got smaller and smaller. They were forced to move farther and farther away from the Wisconsin land they loved.

Some Ho-Chunk families tried to return to Wisconsin. They were turned away by government officials. It would be many years before the Ho-Chunk were welcomed back to their land.

Of the 8.6 million acres of Ho-Chunk land in 1825, a little more than 9,000 acres remain in Wisconsin today.

A new season was beginning for Juliette and John as well. During the previous year, John's family had purchased more land in the growing town of Chicago. John was needed in Chicago to help his family build the growing city.

Life at the fort and on the frontier was changing. Juliette and John made the difficult decision to leave Fort Winnebago to be with John's family in Chicago.

The Ho-Chunk people were saddened by the news. They came in from the surrounding area to ask Juliette and John to stay. "Never, never shall I find such friends again," Elizabeth said.

Juliette was heartbroken. On the morning of July 1, 1833, she and John loaded a boat with their belongings.

Juliette held her young son, Wolcott, in her arms and said goodbye to her friends. As their boat slowly sailed away, Juliette looked back at the group on the shore next to Fort Winnebago. She knew they would be leaving each other forever.

The Historic Indian Agency House

After Juliette and John left Fort Winnebago in 1833, a new Indian Agent moved in. He lived in the Indian Agency House until 1834. After he moved away, the house was used as a trading post, a boarding house, and even a tavern.

Almost 100 years later, the house was still standing, but it was badly damaged and needed repair. People who were interested in history wanted to preserve such an important place. In 1932, a group of women called the National Society of Colonial Dames in the State of Wisconsin purchased the house and restored it. The house was placed on the National Register of Historic Places in 1972.

HISTORIC INDIAN AGENCY HOUSE, DELLA NOHL

The Historic Indian Agency House was restored to its original condition.

Thanks to the Colonial Dames' hard work, the Historic Indian Agency House is one of the oldest remaining homes in Wisconsin. Over the years, people interested in

HISTORIC INDIAN AGENCY HOUSE

Today, the Historic Indian Agency House offers tours and educational programs to the public.

preserving historic buildings have worked to paint, fix, and restore the house and the grounds surrounding it. Today the house is furnished with items similar to what Juliette owned and used. The house looks much like it appeared in Juliette's time.

Today, you can visit the Historic Indian Agency House and see how Juliette and John Kinzie once lived.

11

Beginning of a "New Day"

Their move to Chicago marked a new chapter in the Kinzies' lives. After Juliette and John settled into their new home, they had 6 more children. Juliette and John quickly became 2 of Chicago's leading **citizens**.

Juliette with her daughter Eleanor in 1838, 5 years after the family moved from Fort Winnebago to Chicago

The city of Chicago was growing quickly. The Kinzie family was an important part of the city's growth. John soon became the Indian Agent for the Chicago area. Later he became

citizen (**sit** uh zuhn): a person who lives in a particular place

president of the Village of Chicago. Today, Chicago is one of the biggest cities in the country.

Juliette's pioneering spirit continued. She helped create a school, a hospital, and a church. She was considered a leading lady of Chicago culture and society.

John Harris Kinzie. After John and Juliette left Fort Winnebago, John became a successful businessman in Chicago.

Juliette Kinzie never forgot her experiences on the frontier.

Since moving to Chicago, Juliette had witnessed rapid change in the United States. In less than 25 years, the ways of life for both Indians and non-Indian settlers on the wild frontier had almost entirely disappeared.

Twenty-two years after Juliette and John left Fort Winnebago, the area around the fort looked very different. By 1855, Portage, Wisconsin, was a growing city.

New treaties had moved the Indians off of their lands. The land was now owned by settlers instead of being shared by Indians. Roads were built through the wilderness, making it easier for people to move to new areas. More settlers from the East were moving in and creating cities.

In 1856, when Juliette was 50 years old, she wrote a book about her experiences. She wanted to make sure the stories of the wilderness and the lives of those who shared it would not be forgotten. Juliette called her book, *Wau-Bun: The Early Day in the North-West*. *Wau-Bun* was the Ojibwe word for "new day."

Juliette knew she had lived through an important period of change. She wanted others to know what it was like. Juliette had witnessed Indians using stories to share knowledge from one generation to the next. She hoped her own story would preserve the lives of the early settlers and Indians for generations to come.

Many years later, experts would write about what happened during this time. But Juliette saw these events with her own eyes. She believed an important part of history could be found in the actual experiences and stories of the people who lived it—people like her.

You, too, can write a chapter in our history. Every day there are people, events, and choices that determine the future. You can be a careful observer like Juliette. Think about what you see and hear. Write it down and share it with others. You might have an important story to tell, too—just like Juliette.

Juliette Gordon Low and the Girl Scouts of America

Juliette Kinzie had a personality that inspired people. Juliette's oldest daughter, Eleanor, loved her mother's spirit. Eleanor named her own daughter after Juliette. The young Juliette carried on her grandmother's pioneering spirit and life of adventure.

Young Juliette admired her grandmother's can-do attitude, her love of the outdoors, and her service to others. Like her grandmother, she believed girls could be just as smart and self-sufficient as boys. She believed girls could enjoy camping outdoors, learning new skills, and helping the community. It was no surprise that young Juliette would grow up to become Juliette Gordon Low, the woman who founded the Girl Scouts of America.

Juliette Gordon Low created the Girl Scouts of America to encourage girls to be as capable, resourceful, and kind as her famous grandmother. Some people think the design of

Juliette Gordon Low, Juliette's granddaughter and founder of the Girl Scouts of America

the early Girl Scout uniform was inspired by Juliette Kinzie's life on the frontier.

Appendix

Juliette's Time Line

1806 — Juliette Magill is born in the prosperous town of Middletown, Connecticut.

1820 — Juliette receives a letter from her uncle, Dr. Alexander Wolcott, describing his adventures in the Northwest Territory.

1821 — Juliette moves to Troy, New York, to attend Emma Willard's Troy Female Seminary.

1823 — Juliette's Uncle Alexander Wolcott returns for a visit, bringing along a young friend named John Harris Kinzie. Juliette and John meet.

1830 — Juliette and John marry at Juliette's parents' house.

Juliette and John make the long journey from the East Coast to Detroit, and then to Fort Winnebago, in present-day Portage, Wisconsin.

1831 — Juliette and John move into the blacksmith's log cabin while their home is being built.

After a long, cold winter, Juliette and John travel by horseback to visit John's family in Chicago.

1832 — The Black Hawk War begins.

Juliette and other fort residents escape to Green Bay for safety.

The Black Hawk War ends, and the Treaty of 1832 is signed.

Juliette and John move into the new Indian Agency House.

The government's shipment of silver and corn is delayed. The Indians and settlers are hungry.

1833 — Juliette, John, and their young son leave Fort Winnebago and move to Chicago.

1835–1846 — Juliette and John have 6 more children.

1848 — Wisconsin becomes a state.

1856 — Juliette writes *Wau-Bun: The Early Day in the North-West.*

1860 — Juliette's granddaughter, Juliette Magill Kinzie Gordon, is born. Little Juliette will grow up to become the founder of the Girl Scouts of America.

1870 — Juliette Magill Kinzie dies at the age of 64 while visiting her daughter in New York.

Glossary

Pronunciation Key

a cat (kat), plaid (plad), half (haf)

ah father (**fah** THur), heart (hahrt)

air carry (**kair** ee), bear (bair), where (whair)

aw all (awl), law (law), bought (bawt)

ay say (say), break (brayk), vein (vayn)

e bet (bet), says (sez), deaf (def)

ee bee (bee), team (teem), fear (feer)

i bit (bit), women (**wim** uhn), build (bild)

ı ice (ıs), lie (lı), sky (skı)

o hot (hot), watch (wotch)

oh open (**oh** puhn), sew (soh)

oi boil (boil), boy (boi)

oo pool (pool), move (moov), shoe (shoo)

or order (**or** dur), more (mor)

ou house (hous), now (nou)

u good (gud), should (shud)

uh cup (kuhp), flood (fluhd), button (**buht** uhn)

ur burn (burn), pearl (purl), bird (burd)

yoo use (yooz), few (fyoo), view (vyoo)

hw what (hwuht), when (hwen)

TH that (THat), breathe (breeTH)

zh measure (**mezh** ur), garage (guh **razh**)

113

American Revolutionary War: the war for American independence from Great Britain, fought from 1775 to 1783

ammunition (am yuh **nish** uhn): objects fired from weapons

annual: happening once a year

astonished (uh **ston** isht): to strike with sudden wonder or surprise

ceremony (**ser** uh moh nee): an act performed in some regular way according to fixed rules especially as part of a social or religious event

citizen (**sit** uh zuhn): a person who lives in a particular place

continent: one of the great divisions of land on the globe—Africa, Antarctica, Asia, Australia, Europe, North America, or South America

convenience (kuhn **vee** nyuns): personal comfort

cooperation (koh op uh **ray** suhn): the act or process of working together to get something done

culture: the habits, beliefs, and traditions of a particular people, place, or time

custom: the usual way of doing things

deprived (di **prɪvd**): to take something away from or keep from having something

desolate (**des** uh lit): without signs of life

destination (des tuh **nay** shuhn): a place to which a person is going or something is sent

discouraged (dis **kur** ijd): made to feel less determined, hopeful, or confident

dispute: an argument or disagreement

document: to record the details about

drafty: having usually cool air moving through

eagerly (**ee** gur lee): very excited and interested

eerie (**ir** ee): causing fear and uneasiness

epidemic (ep uh **dem** ik): a rapidly spreading outbreak of disease

etiquette (**et** uh ket): the rules governing the proper way to behave or to do something

expand: to grow or increase in size

expensive (ek **spen** siv): costly

fashionable: following current fashion or style

fawn: a young deer

frontier (fruhn **tir**): the edge of a settled part of a country

glade: an open space in a forest

headdress (**hed** dres): a covering or ornament for the head

heartbroken: overcome by sorrow

husk: the outer covering of a fruit or seed

interpreter (in **tur** pruh tur): a person who turns spoken words of one language into a different language

journey: an act of traveling from one place to another

lacrosse (luh **kraws**): a game played on a field using a long-handled stick with a shallow net for catching, throwing, and carrying the ball

magnificent (mag **nif** uh suhnt): very beautiful or impressive

massacre (**mas** uh kur): the violent and cruel killing of a large number of people

messenger: a person who carries a message or does an errand

militia (muh **li** shuh): a group of citizens with military training who are called into service in emergencies

mournful: full of sorrow or sadness

negotiated (ni **go** shee ay tid): to have a discussion with another in order to settle something

Northwest Territory: a large part of the United States that once included all or parts of Indiana, Illinois, Michigan, Wisconsin, and Minnesota

passenger: someone riding on or in a vehicle

pioneer: a person who is one of the first to settle in an area or to do something new

plea: an earnest appeal

policy: a set of guidelines or rules that determine how something is done

prestige (pre **steezh**): importance or respect gained through success or excellence

rhythm (**riᴛʜ** uhm): a regular repeated pattern of beats, sounds, activity, or movements

routine (roo **teen**): a usual order and way of doing something

settler: a person who comes to live in a new region

social status: position or rank in a particular society

staple: something that is used widely and often

toiling: to work hard and long

treaty: an agreement between 2 or more states or groups of people

vast: very great in size or amount

venison: the meat of a deer used for food

Reading Group Guide and Activities

Discussion Questions

❧ Juliette Kinzie lived at a time when women had fewer rights than men. She believed men and women should have the same opportunities. List examples of Juliette's beliefs from the text. Why did Juliette believe she could "survive on the frontier as well as any man?"

❧ Juliette and John spent a lot of time traveling. Think about the trips you have taken. How did you travel? How long did it take? What dangers did you face? Compare and contrast your journey with Juliette and John's experiences.

❧ Treaties between the US government and Indians have been described as a game where only one side knows the rules. Imagine what that feels like. If one side knows the rules and one side doesn't, how can that change the outcome? Juliette thought many of the treaties with the local tribes were unfair. Can you think of a way to make a treaty process fair?

Activities

❧ Juliette Kinzie stood up for the Indians. She supported their rights to have their own beliefs and their own land. Think about different times in your own life when you stood up for someone else. Think about the times when someone else stood up for you. How would you have acted in Juliette's shoes? Create a panel cartoon that illustrates the scenario.

Juliette took notes and drew sketches that described her surroundings. She also wrote about what she did and the people she met. Try keeping your own journal. Describe your own surroundings. What do you do each day? Who are your friends? Where do you go? What do you eat for meals? After several days or weeks, read back over your journal. What themes or patterns do you see? What do you think someone in the future might learn from your observations?

The US government wanted settlers to move to the western lands. How do you think they would get people interested in moving to this new location? Create an advertisement, poster, or commercial from either Juliette's or the US government's point of view. Your goal is to convince pioneers from the East to settle on the new frontier. How might Juliette's ad be different from the government's?

Learn more about the impact women have had on Wisconsin history. Read the Badger Biographies of Dr. Kate Pelham Newcomb and Belle Case La Follette. Imagine a conversation among Juliette, Dr. Kate, and Belle. What do you think they would say to each other? What did they have in common? How did their experiences differ? If you could ask them any question, what would it be? Write a script for you and some friends and act out the conversation. Have fun with it!

To Learn More about Indian Life in Wisconsin

Holliday, Diane Young. *Mountain Wolf Woman: A Ho-Chunk Girlhood*. Madison: Wisconsin Historical Society Press, 2007.

Hunter, Sally M. *Four Seasons of Corn: A Winnebago Tradition*. Minneapolis: Lerner, 1996.

Loew, Patty. *Native People of Wisconsin*. Madison: Wisconsin Historical Society Press, 2003.

Shemie, Bonnie. *Houses of Bark: Tipi, Wigwam And Longhouse*. Montreal: Tundra Books, 1990.

Acknowledgments

My relationship with Juliette Kinzie began when I was a child. A fourth grade class on the history of Chicago piqued my interest, which went into overdrive once I learned our local cemetery held the remains of a "real life" pioneer. Thus began a lifelong quest for seeing places and times past through the eyes of others.

I want to thank Bobbie Malone, retired director of the Wisconsin Historical Society's Office of School Services, for recognizing my excitement for Juliette's story and suggesting I share it in this Badger Biography. It has been my joy and pleasure. Thanks also to Destinee Udelhoven, director of the Historic Indian Agency House, for her encouragement and assistance, and to the National Society of Colonial Dames in the State of Wisconsin for their caring stewardship of the Indian Agency House.

Thank you to Bill Cronon for his advice and guidance, and to historian Peter Shrake and Bill Quackenbush of the Ho-Chunk Nation for their careful review of the manuscript. I want to thank the Girl Scouts of America, especially Katherine Keena, director of the Juliette Gordon Low Birthplace, for her excitement about Juliette's legacy and for sharing the lovely portraits that grace this book.

I appreciate and thank the talented efforts of Wisconsin Historical Society Press Director Kathy Borkowski and editor Carrie Kilman. Carrie's enthusiastic guidance and skillful editing helped shape the story you read today.

I must express heartfelt thanks to my family for their loving embrace of Juliette Kinzie in our lives. From my husband's suggestion that we hop in the car and spend spring break retracing Juliette's infamous trip from Fort Winnebago to Chicago, to my daughters' scrounging for artifacts in the museum archives, Juliette has become part of our extended family.

And finally, to the Kinzie women and the many storytellers who have followed in their footsteps, thank you.

Index

This index points you to the pages where you can read about persons, places, and ideas. If you do not find the word you are looking for, try to think of another word that means about the same thing.

When you see a page number in **bold** it means there is a picture on that page.